IT'S TIME TO EAT APPLESAUCE

It's Time to Eat APPLESAUCE

Walter the Educator

Silent King Books
A WhichHead Entertainment Imprint

Copyright © 2024 by Walter the Educator

All rights reserved. No part of this book may be reproduced in any manner whatsoever without written per- mission except in the case of brief quotations embodied in critical articles and reviews.

First Printing, 2024

Disclaimer

This book is a literary work; the story is not about specific persons, locations, situations, and/or circumstances unless mentioned in a historical context. Any resemblance to real persons, locations, situations, and/or circumstances is coincidental. This book is for entertainment and informational purposes only. The author and publisher offer this information without warranties expressed or implied. No matter the grounds, neither the author nor the publisher will be accountable for any losses, injuries, or other damages caused by the reader's use of this book. The use of this book acknowledges an understanding and acceptance of this disclaimer.

It's Time to Eat APPLESAUCE is a collectible early learning book by Walter the Educator suitable for all ages belonging to Walter the Educator's Time to Eat Book Series. Collect more books at WaltertheEducator.com

USE THE EXTRA SPACE TO TAKE NOTES AND DOCUMENT YOUR MEMORIES

APPLESAUCE

It's time to eat, come gather 'round,

It's Time to Eat
Applesauce

A tasty treat is to be found.

What's in the bowl, so smooth and sweet?

Applesauce! Oh, what a treat!

Golden, shiny, soft and bright,

A spoonful brings such pure delight.

It's made from apples, ripe and true,

Mashed and cooked just right for you.

The scent is warm, like autumn air,

With cinnamon, it's even fair!

A little spice, a little sweet,

Applesauce is fun to eat!

Dip in your spoon, give it a try,

It's soft and yummy, oh, don't be shy!

Swish it around, take a big bite,

Applesauce makes everything right.

It's Time to Eat
Applesauce

It's good at lunch or as a snack,

You'll love it more with every smack.

It's smooth and cool, it's never rough,

One bowl's just never enough!

From orchards tall, where apples grow,

To kitchens warm, where cooks all know,

Applesauce is the best by far,

Like eating sunshine from a jar.

You can eat it plain or mix it in,

A perfect way the fun begins.

Top your pancakes, or swirl it fast,

Applesauce makes each meal a blast!

It's great for kids, and grown-ups too,

A treat that's healthy, just for you.

It makes you smile, it's always nice,

It's Time to Eat
Applesauce

And only needs one spoon, not twice!

So scoop it up, don't let it wait,

This applesauce is simply great.

A bowl of joy, a taste so pure,

It's time to eat, that's for sure!

When the bowl is empty, don't be blue,

There's always more, just make some new!

With applesauce, the fun won't end,

It's Time to Eat
Applesauce

It's a tasty treat and a yummy friend!

ABOUT THE CREATOR

Walter the Educator is one of the pseudonyms for Walter Anderson. Formally educated in Chemistry, Business, and Education, he is an educator, an author, a diverse entrepreneur, and he is the son of a disabled war veteran. "Walter the Educator" shares his time between educating and creating. He holds interests and owns several creative projects that entertain, enlighten, enhance, and educate, hoping to inspire and motivate you. Follow, find new works, and stay up to date with Walter the Educator™

at WaltertheEducator.com

www.ingramcontent.com/pod-product-compliance
Lightning Source LLC
LaVergne TN
LVHW052010060526
838201LV00059B/3953